Getty Kids Hymnal
Hymns from Home

T0085689

Table of Contents

All Things Bright and Beautiful

Words by Horatio G. Spafford
Music by Philip P. Bliss
Arranged by Keith Getty
and Fionán de Barra

Christ Our Hope in Life and Death

Words and Music by
Keith Getty, Matt Boswell, Jordan Kauflin,
Matt Merker and Matt Papa

Christ Our Hope in Life and Death

4

Christ Our Hope in Life and Death

sing hal - le - lu - jah! Now and ev - er we con - fess Christ our hope in life and death. Now and ev - er we con - fess Christ our hope in life and death.

Great is Thy Faithfulness

Music by William M. Runyan
Words by Thomas O. Chisholm
Arranged by Keith Getty
and Fionán de Barra

Arrangement © 2021 Getty Music Publishing (BMI) / Fionán de Barra (BMI) (adm. at MusicServices.org)

Great is Thy Faithfulness

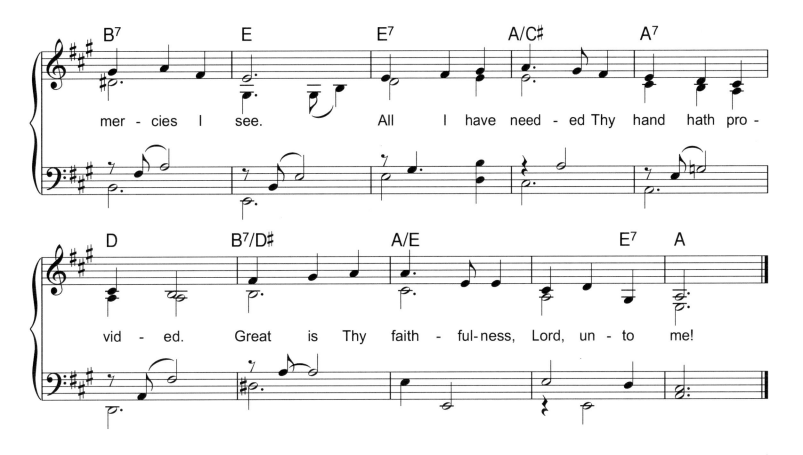

mer - cies I see. All I have need - ed Thy hand hath pro - vid - ed. Great is Thy faith - ful-ness, Lord, un - to me!

For the Beauty of the Earth

Words by Folliott S. Pierpoint
Music by Conrad Kocher
Arranged by Keith Getty
and Fionán de Barra

Christ the Lord is Risen Today

Words by Charles Wesley
Tune: Easter Hymn (Lyra Davidica, 1708)
Arranged by Keith Getty
and Fionán de Barra

1. Christ the Lord is ris'n to - day,___
2. Love's re - deem - ing work is done,___
3. Lives a - gain our glo - rious King,___
4. Soar we now where Christ has led,___

Al - le - lu - ia!

Earth and heav'n in cho - rus say,___
Fought the fight, the bat - tle won,___
Where, O death, is now thy sting?_
Fol - l'wing our ex - al - ted Head,___

Al - le - lu - ia!

Raise your joys and tri - umphs high,
Death in vain for - bids him rise,
Once he died our souls to save,
Made like him, like him we rise,

Al - le - lu - ia!

Sing, ye heav'ns, and earth rep - ly,___
Christ has o - pened pa - ra - dise,___
Where's thy vic - t'ry, boast - ing grave?_
Ours_ the cross, the grave, the skies,___

Al - le - lu - ia!

Amazing Grace

Music by Trad.
Words by John Newton
Arranged by Keith Getty
and Fionán de Barra

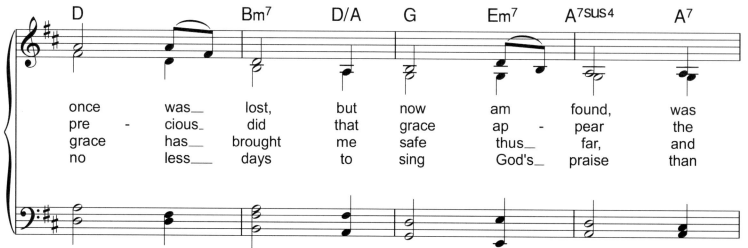

Amazing Grace

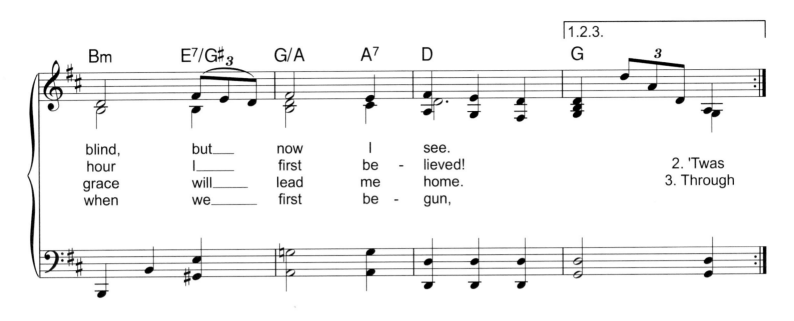

blind, but___ now I see.
hour I___ first be - lieved!
grace will___ lead me home.
when we___ first be - gun,

2. 'Twas
3. Through

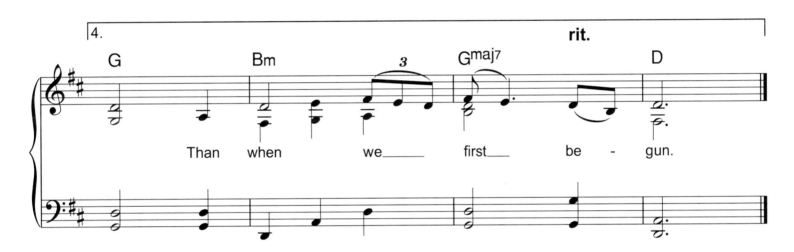

Than when we___ first___ be - gun.

A Mighty Fortress Is Our God

Words and Music by
Martin Luther ('Ein Feste Burg')
Trans. by Frederick H. Hedge
Arranged by Keith Getty
and Fionán de Barra

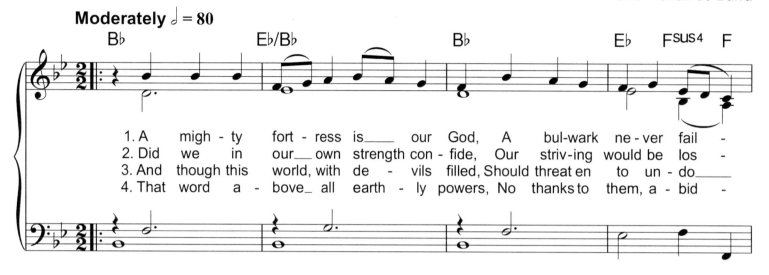

A Mighty Fortress Is Our God

It Is Well with My Soul

Words by Horatio G. Spafford
Music by Philip P. Bliss
Arranged by Keith Getty
and Fionán de Barra

It Is Well

Refrain

soul. (with my soul.) It is well, it is well with my soul._____

And Can It Be?

Music by Thomas Campbell
Words by Charles Wesley
Arranged by Keith Getty
and Fionán de Barra

Gently (♩ = 70)

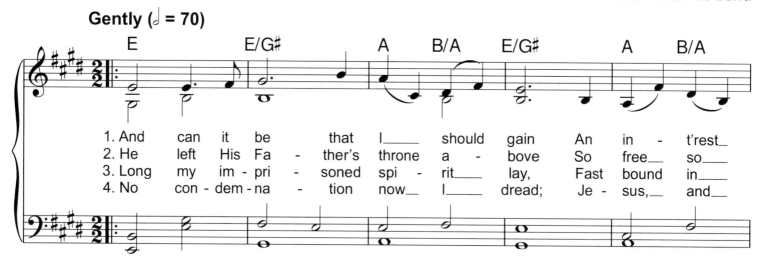

1. And can it be that I____ should gain An in - t'rest____
2. He left His Fa - ther's throne a - bove So free____ so____
3. Long my im - pri - soned spi - rit____ lay, Fast bound in____
4. No con - dem - na - tion now__ I____ dread; Je - sus,__ and__

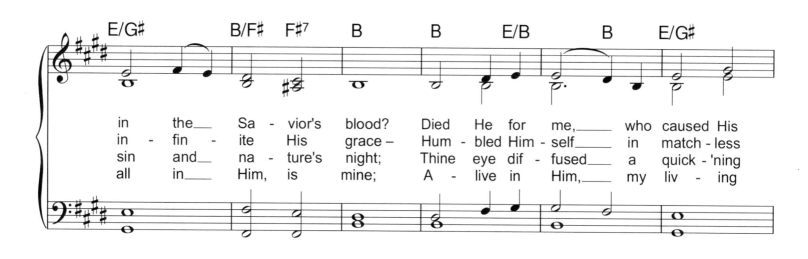

in the__ Sa - vior's blood? Died He for me,____ who caused His
in - fin - ite His grace – Hum - bled Him - self____ in match - less
sin and__ na - ture's night; Thine eye dif - fused____ a quick - 'ning
all in__ Him, is mine; A - live in Him,____ my liv - ing

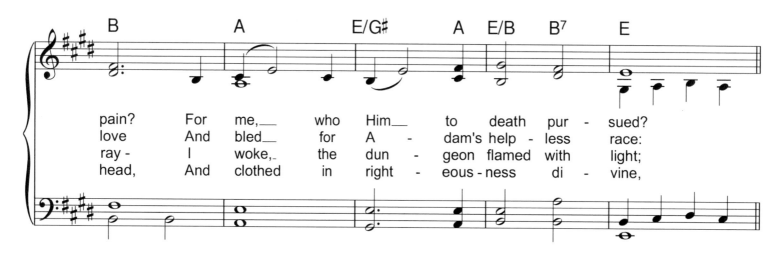

pain? For me,__ who Him__ to death pur - sued?
love And bled__ for A - dam's help - less race:
ray - I woke,__ the dun - geon flamed with light;
head, And clothed in right - eous - ness di - vine,

And Can It Be?

"**He** established a testimony in Jacob
and appointed a law in Israel,
which he commanded our fathers
to teach to their children,
that the next generation might know them,
the children yet unborn,
and arise and tell them to their children,
so that they should set their hope in God..."

Psalm 78:5-7 (ESV)

We have left the last pages empty just for you, so that you can try writing your very own hymns...

Revive Us Again / Blessed Assurance

Words by Fanny J. Crosby
Music by Phoebe P. Knapp
Arranged by Keith Getty
and Fionán de Barra

To Refrain

CODA

scat - tered our night. All glo - ry and praise To the Lamb that was slain, who has
path's dai - ly light. Re - vive us a - gain, Fill each heart with Thy love, may each

borne all our sins and has cleansed ev -'ry stain.
soul be re - kin - dled with fire from a - bove.
Hal - le

- gain.

With Energy (♩. = 60)

1. Bless - ed as - sur - ance, Je - sus is mine: O what a
2. Per - fect sub - miss - ion, all is at rest, I in my

fore - taste of glo - ry di - vine! Heir of sal - va - tion, pur - chase of
Sav - ior am hap - py and blest; Watch - ing and wait - ing, look - ing a -

20

My Heart is Filled with Thankfulness

Words and Music by Keith Getty
and Stuart Townend

Lilting (♩ = 90)
Dmaj7 A E/G♯ F♯m7 D A/C♯ F♯m7
1. My heart is filled with thank - ful - ness to Him who bore my
2. My heart is filled with thank - ful - ness to Him who walks be -
3. My heart is filled with thank - ful - ness to Him who reigns a -
Dadd9 A F♯m7 E D A/C♯ Esus4
pain; who plumbed the depths of my dis - grace and gave me life a -
side; who floods my weak-ness - es with strength and caus-es fears to
bove; whose wis - dom is my per - fect peace, whose ev - ery thought is
A Asus4 A F♯m7 A/E D E F♯m D A/C♯
gain. Who crushed my curse of sin - ful - ness and clothed me in His
fly. Whose ev - ery pro - mise is e - nough for ev - ery step I
love. For ev - ery day I have on earth is gi - ven by the
Esus4 E A F♯m7 E D A/C♯ Esus4
light and wrote His law of right-eous-ness with pow'r u - pon my
take; sus - tain - ing me with arms of love and crown-ing me with
King. So I will give my life, my all, to love and fol - low

My Heart is Filled with Thankfulness

Sing We the Song of Emmanuel

Words and Music by
Matt Boswell, Matt Papa,
Stuart Townend and Keith Getty

Tag (3rd time: opt. acapella)

25

Sing We the Song of Emmanuel

(Title)

Written by _____

(Title)

Written by _____